LOS ANGELES
AND ORANGE COUNTIES

GREATER

LOS ANGELES

Text by
ATTILIO L. DE ALBERI
Photos by
ANDREA PISTOLESI

EB
BONECHI

© Copyright 1994 by Casa Editrice Bonechi, via Cairoli 18/b - 50131 Florence - Italy
Tel. 39/55/576841 - Telex 571323 CEB - Fax 39/55/5000766

Text by ATTILIO L. DE ALBERI
Photographs from the Archives of Casa Editrice Bonechi taken by ANDREA PISTOLESI.
Pages 55, 56: photographs by Stefano Cellai.
Pages 78, 79: © The Walt Disney Company.
The Publisher thanks the Universal Studios *and the* Walt Disney Company *for their kind cooperation.*

ISBN 88-8029-178-5

* * *

INTRODUCTION

GREATER LOS ANGELES

"It's so big!" "It's so spread out!" exclaim first time visitors to Los Angeles. And rightly so. The immediate thing to realize about Los Angeles is that it is not a city, at least according to the European definition: a community with a defined "historical" center where people both live and work. "Six suburbs in Search of a City" is one of the descriptions given to this vast metropolis - or, more correctly, megalopolis - extending itself for more than 464 square miles between the mountains and the Pacific Ocean and containing residential, business and pleasure areas. The Big Orange, L.A., Tinseltown, La-La Land, the City of Angels, or even Lost Angels is how Los Angeles is also known and it seems to confirm both the variety of locale and the fact that this city can be different things to different people.

It was October 1542 when Portuguese explorer Juan Cabrillo landed on the shores of what is today, Greater Los Angeles. At that time the local population numbered some 4000 Native Americans of about 30 tribes. But it was only 200 years later, on August 2, 1769 to be exact, that Fra Juan Crespi, chronicler for Gaspar de Portola's 50-men expedition travelling north from San Diego (site of the first Spanish Franciscan mission), called the river by the ancient Indian village of Yang-na, Río de Nuestra Señora la Reina de Los Angeles de Porciúncula. Real settlement, however, did not start until a decade later, and the Pueblo of Los Angeles, as it came to be known, was not established officially until 1781. Nothing much really happened to this community of ranchers even after Alta California became part of newly independent Mexico in 1821. But soon after the whole region was ceded to the United States in 1848, the Gold Rush hit California and although San Francisco was the queen of the 'epidemic,' all the miners and explorers in the north had to be fed. The fortune of Los Angeles ranchers, who could sell cattle up to $435 a head, was made very quickly. On May 10, 1869, the Central Pacific and the Union Pacific laid the last tracks of the cross-country railroad and a major step was taken in uniting California with the rest of the nation. By 1885 the competition between the Southern Pacific and the Santa Fe companies had grown so fierce that train

The world-famous Hollywood sign on the Hollywood Hills. In the background, to the north, the vast expanse of the San Fernando Valley, also known, simply, as "the Valley." Up to the 1930s the valley was practically a vast series of orange groves and orchards. The housing development is a relatively recent phenomenon.

An aerial view of the intersection between the 10 and 110 Freeways. In the background Downtown Los Angeles.

fares dropped and one could travel from the Mississippi River to Los Angeles for only $1! Waves after waves of homesteaders started flowing from the Mid-West and from the East as a series of 'booms' hit this sleepy and isolated Californian town of only 10,000 people.

First it was the Orange Boom, when vast citrus belts were planted to satisfy the ever-growing demand of cities such as New York and Boston. The newcomers of the post-Civil War era brought money with them and soon an investment and real estate boom ensued. By the turn of the century electric trolley cars connected newly-formed communities, a 14-story skyscraper dominated the center and automobile registration totaled 20,000. By 1910, the population had grown to 200,000 and in 1920, just before the discovery of oil and the subsequent boom, Los Angeles surpassed San Francisco dwelling to 500,000 inhabitants. At the end

of the roaring twenties Los Angeles was a modern world city and in 1932 its prestige grew immensely when it hosted the Olympic Games.

In this same period, another phenomenon was taking place, destined to change the role of Los Angeles in the world - the irresistible growth of the movie industry. Shortly after the beginning of the century, many movie producers moved their operations from the East Coast to escape the monopoly of Thomas Edison and its eight partners in the Motion Picture Patents Co., and to take advantage of the year-round sunny weather which was more suitable for outdoor filming. The variety of nearby ocean, mountain, countryside, city and desert offered a splendid choice of locations. It was in the small community of Hollywood, then just outside Los Angeles, that some vacant barns were first utilized to process films shot around town. Pretty soon entire sets and movie studios were created, attracting talent from all parts of America and the world. The Golden Age of Hollywood peaked in 1939, the year in which "Gone with the Wind" hit the screens. After World War II the movies had to confront a new competitor - television - and learn how to cohabit with it. Yet this new development did not take away much from Los Angeles but actually confirmed - along with the growth of the record industry - the status of this city as the Entertainment Capital of the World. Hollywood is the second most important U.S. industry in terms of exports. The first one is aviation. Both of them are based in the Los Angeles Basin. And yet the Aviation Boom, which exploded during World War II and continued well after 1945, was not the last one to favour Los Angeles. The flourishing of allied electronics and computer industries was soon to take place, followed by an expansion in banking, clothing manufacture (especially sportswear) and finance. Today, Los Angeles is home to the Pacific Stock Exchange, while Long Beach-San Pedro is one of the biggest ports on the Pacific coast of the Americas. As the world economy moves towards the Pacific Rim, this city increasingly becomes one of its major players. Another impressive feature of this city with an urbanized population now surpassing 11.5 million, is the immense variety of ethnic groups which have made their home here - well beyond the blonde, tanned and athletic stereotype depicted in films and television. This cultural mosaic is reflected in the incredible range of different cuisines available to choose from. As Los Angeles moves fast towards the 21st century, you are invited to explore with us this immense Babel of peoples, this "salad bowl" of unforgettable attractions and cultural stimuli.

An aerial view of Santa Monica with its beach and pier.

An aerial view of Downtown Los Angeles: the skyscrapers of Bunker Hill. The tallest structure at the center is the First Interstate World Center; to the right the Gas Company Tower; to the left the 444 Plaza Building (location for the famous L.A. Law TV show), projecting its shadow onto the "new" Central Library. In the immediate foreground the tower of the recently renovated Biltmore Hotel.

A general view of the Downtown Los Angeles' skyline, from the south. In the background from left to right the Hollywood Hills and the San Gabriel Mountains.

THE HEART OF DOWNTOWN

Does Los Angeles have a downtown or center? To many people (including many Angelenos) the answer is no. Critics of this megalopolis claim that it does not have a heart, or a central core. They see Los Angeles as no more than a sum of suburbs, with inhabitants on four wheels moving swiftly from one suburb to another, impervious to urban integration. But there is a Downtown in Los Angeles, roughly bounded by Temple Street on the north, Olympic Boulevard on the south, and Alameda and Figueroa on the east and west, respectively. Although the smallest of any major American city, the center still reflects L.A.'s remarkable urban variety through the kaleidoscope of its mini-districts.

Historically Los Angeles began in and around the **Old Plaza** and **Olvera Street**, but later development and growth pushed the heart of the city to another area, approximately seven blocks west, on **Pershing Square**. Opening onto the square (where a new

massive program of restoration and beautification, offering it a "21st century look," has just just been completed), the deluxe **Biltmore Hotel** was built. By the late 19th century **Bunker Hill** was lined by elegant residences, and the mansions could be reached by **Angels' Flight**, a unique type of cable car soon to be restored.

But when the fear of earthquakes inspired city planners to prohibit buildings more than 150 feet high, many companies started to head out along **Wilshire Boulevard** (a stretch going all the way to the Pacific Ocean) and other outlying areas. It was then that Los Angeles started growing horizontally, rather than vertically. Thanks to the advancement in construction techniques, the old ban on tall buildings was finally removed by the year 1957 and a new Renaissance benefited Downtown culminating with the development boom of the '80s. Nowadays the visitor can enjoy the majesty of its impressive skyline made of concrete, steel and most especially mirror-

7

The mirror-glass cylinders of the Westin Bonaventure Hotel.

Another view of the Bonaventure Hotel *from across the Harbor Freeway. To the left, the sun hits the mirror-glass surface of the* Sheraton Grand Hotel; *behind it the* 52 *story Security Pacific National Bank Building.*

The mirror -glass surface of the Sheraton Grand Hotel.

A view of Downtown from across the Harbor Freeway. The Union Bank Building *in the foreground.*

glass. It is a spectacle not to miss, particularly at sunset, when the last rays of the day coming from the ocean hit the polished surfaces of the many skyscrapers. Or, if you happen to be in Los Angeles during the winter, you might enjoy the magnificent view of the Downtown skyline with a background of the snow-covered San Gabriel mountains.
Although Downtown is served by minibuses, by a fleet of taxis and, more recently by the newly built Red Line subway, the best way to enjoy its richness is to leave the car behind and walk. A full tour will take approximately half a day.
Starting from **Pershing Square**, which provides several levels of underground parking, you might want to go and visit the **International Jewelry Center** on the south-east corner of Hill and Sixth Street. The way this modern structure has been built allows jewelers to take advantage of the northern light, supposedly the best in which to examine fine gems. More shops and offices of Los Angeles' large

The stair-shaped sculpture "Double Ascension" by Herbert Bazer, on the Arco Center Plaza, by night.

Two different views of the 444 Plaza roof-top garden by night.

Following pages:
a striking general view of Downtown Los Angeles at dusk. The last rays of the sun coming from the Pacific Ocean illuminate the top parts of the skyscrapers.

jewelry trade can be found one block down on Hill Street. Always in the same area, at 616 Olive Street, it is worthwhile to see the **Oviatt Building**, certainly one of Los Angeles' most significant examples of Art Deco architecture and once a prestigious men's clothier with clients such as Rudolph Valentino and Douglas Fairbanks. Not to be missed is its beautiful entrance, created by French designer René Lalique. In place of the clothing store today there is the **Rex Restaurant**, appropriately decorated as a 1920 ocean liner.

On Olive you can walk north to the **Biltmore Hotel**, between Sixth and Fifth Street. The recent multi-million renovation has brought back the splendor of its early days in the 1920s. You might want to walk up the wrought-iron balustrades of the central staircase, past the wonderful Spanish Renaissance lobby and onto the Galleria level, from which you can catch a glimpse of famous meeting rooms such as the Music Room, the Gold Room and the Grand Ballroom.

You can actually reach 5th street going through the hotel and you find yourself facing the eastern side of the **Los Angeles Central Library**, recently re-opened to the public after two tragic arson fires in 1986. Its historic 1926 pyramid-tower Goodhue Building, has been restored to its original state, with dazzling architecture, sculptures and inscriptions reflecting the theme, "the light of learning." A new, impressive modern wing has also been added. The "new" Central Library, with its 2.1 million books, 10,000 magazine subscriptions and over 2 million historic photographs is the third largest library in the nation.

At this point of your tour you might be ready to leave the past, however restored, and immerse yourself in the imposing beauty of a thoroughly modern center of skyscrapers, decorated lobbies, pensile gardens, fountains, sculptures, escalators and pedestrian bridges, stopping for an espresso or cappuccino, or a light snack, served in many of the little cafes of the area frequented mainly by corporate executives, attorneys, financial wizards and banking experts.

Right across from the Central Library's eastern gardens on Flower Street, you can reach the **Arco**

Pedestrian Bridge coming out of the World Trade Center. *Pedestrian bridges like this one are a regular feature in the Downtown business district, and often allow you to pass from one block to another without stepping foot on the streets.*

California Plaza.

444 Plaza Building.

The sculpture "Mind, Body and Spirit" by Gidon Graetz. To the left the Wells Fargo Center. *To the right the* Great Western Bank Building.

From the bottom of Grand Avenue towards the skies: the Wells Fargo Center *to the left and the twin* California Plaza towers *to he right.*

Towers and Center, forming a plaza brightened by Herbert Bazer's stair-shaped sculpture **"Double Ascension."** From here you can take the outside escalator up to the foot-bridge over 5th Street and enter the futuristic structure of the **Westin Bonaventure Hotel,** with its mirrored glass cylinders, six-level open courtyard, glass-capsule elevators and revolving restaurant on the top floor. Across Fourth Street you have the **World Trade Center,** a block-wide enclosed mall with shops dealing in imports and currency-exchange. A pedestrian bridge will take you across Flower Street to the 52 story **Security Pacific National Bank Building** and to the series of plazas, gardens and skyscrapers of **Bunker Hill** proper. On the southern part of the hill you can admire the tallest building on

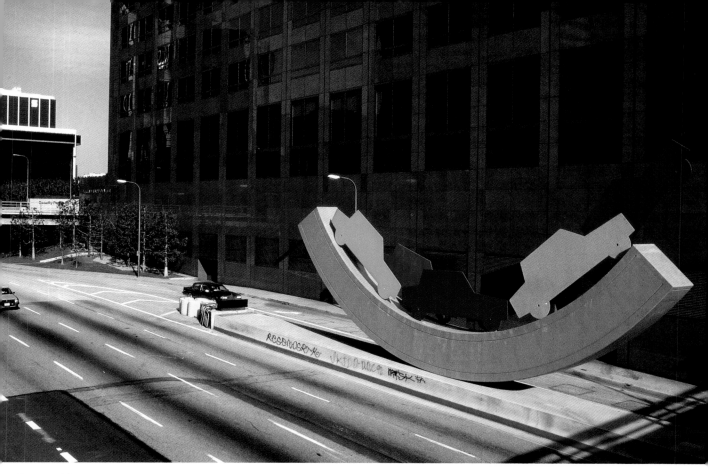

On page 16 top: *aerial view of Downtown Los Angeles from the south-east.*
Bottom: *from left to right: the* Gas Company Tower, *the* First Interstate World Building, California Plaza.

On page 17: *the heart of Downtown at sunset. From left to right: the* First Interstate Tower, 444 Plaza, *the* Security Pacific National Bank Building, *the* First Interstate World Center, *the* Wells Fargo Center *and the* Gas Company Tower.

On page 18 top left: *The sculpture "Mind, body and Spirit" by Gidon Graetz - the* First Interstate World Center *in the background.*
Top Right: *The sculpture "Ulysses" by Alexander Liberman - the* Security Pacific National Bank Building *in the background.*
Bottom left: *Fountain at the entrance of the* Museum of Contemporary Art (MOCA).
Bottom right: *Another view of the "Ulysses" sculpture.*

On page 19: *huge street sculpture on Fourth, by the* Wells Fargo Center, *celebrating one of L.A.'s inescapable features: car traffic.*

the West Coast, the 74 story high **First Interstate World Center**. Its lobby contains giant artwork dedicated to "Our Lady of the Angels of Porciúncula.' The building is flanked by two other giants. To the east is the **Gas Company Tower**. To the west, across the lovely Spanish Steps and a gorgeous roof-top garden adorned with palm-trees, you find the **444 Plaza Building**, location of the famous *L.A.Law* TV series. From the top of the stairs you can walk along Hope Street and at the corner of 4th see, facing each other, the modern sculptures of **Ulysses** by Alexander Liberman and **Mind, Body and Spirit** by Gidon Graetz. To complete your tour of the area you can walk, through the **Crocker Center**, modelled after a glass-walled Victorian-age conservatory, to Grand Avenue onto **California Plaza** with its twin towers. On Grand Avenue, to the north, you will find the **Museum of Contemporary Art (MOCA)**, a red sandstone building enriched by entrancing fountains. At this point of your tour you might be ready to

experience, in an almost shocking fashion, the incredible ethnic and cultural diversity of Los Angeles. Just descend from the futuristic landscape of Bunker Hill and enter the **Grand Central Market** from Hill Street: it is true time-travelling. You can walk through this colorful bazaar of vegetables, fruits and international foods (mostly Mexican and Chinese) and feel you are back to those times when public markets, rather than anonymous supermarkets were the rule. And, if you are thirsty, don't miss the juice stand at the entrance on Hill Street, where the most incredible variety of fresh fruit and vegetable juices are served.
Walking through the Central Market you will end up on **Broadway** where the **Latino commercial district** begins, and you will feel you are no longer in the U.S.A.! And since you are on Broadway, go up towards Third Street and see the **Million Dollar Theater** and enjoy the eccentric exterior of L.A.'s first movie palace (circa 1918).

The Mark Taper Forum theater, *site of some of the best performed plays in town, at the* Music Center.

View of the Music Center's fountain, *with the* Mark Taper Forum *in the background on the left.*

View of the Music Center's Lipchitz's sculpture *(dedicated to peace) and fountain - the* Department of Water and Power building *in the background.*

CIVIC CENTER

Our visit to Downtown will further confirm its splendid variety with a short detour to the **Pacific Stock Exchange**, at 233 South Beaudry Avenue, between 2nd and 3rd Street, right across the **Harbor Freeway.** Here we have a miniature version of the much bigger one in New York City. As a spectator you can observe the often frenzied activities from the visitors' gallery on the 11th floor of the building.

Start a tour of the **Civic Center** - site of all the local government and federal offices, and the courts - by passing through the magnificent **Music Center**, located in an elevated position on one single block between Temple and First Street and most easily accessible from either Hope Street or Grand Avenue.

"What is the difference between L.A. and a bowl of yogurt?" "Well, at least the bowl of yogurt is a ... live culture." The joke reflects an old stereotype about Los Angeles, as some kind of 'cultural desert.' The forty million dollar monument to Los Angeles' performing arts called Music Center, was built in the mid-1960s as a conscious effort to both enrich the 'cultural patina' of the city (often and unfavorably compared to New York) and to revitalize a decaying Downtown.

The largest of the three theaters which make up the complex is the **Dorothy Chandler Pavilion** on the south, home of the Los Angeles Philharmonic Orchestra and hosting the Oscar night extravaganza (or Academy Award Presentations) seen annually by millions of people around the globe thanks to satellite television. Walking across the plaza, highlighted by a large fountain and by Jacques Lipchitz's impressive bronze sculptures, you can reach the **Mark Taper Forum**, a unique circular structure surrounded by a pool, usually featuring contemporary drama. Right behind it, to the north, is the **Ahmanson Theater** host to Civic Light Opera Performances. From the citadel-like Music Center you can have a great view of the various office and court buildings characterizing the Civic Center proper.

Two views of the City Hall tower. *Site of the city's government, the building was the first skyscraper in Los Angeles. Built in the '20s, it is often utilized as a film location.*

Aerial view of City Hall, *surrounded by other government buildings.*

Sculpture at the entrance of Little Tokyo's Japanese Plaza Village, *where you can find many authentic Japanese restaurants and shops.*

CITY HALL - LITTLE JAPAN

From the Music Center we suggest you to stroll down 1st street so that you might visit the old **Los Angeles Times Building**, at the corner of Spring Street. The *L.A Times*,with its daily circulation of more than 1.1 million copies is the second largest newspaper in the country and it is certainly becoming one of the most influential. Tours of the facilities are offered to visitors on Spring Street. One block north of there, you will encounter the ''pearl'' of the Civic Center: **City Hall**. It is interesting to know that this was the only structure to escape, by public vote, the restriction against high buildings. The twenty-eight story high tower was built between 1926-28, and up to 1957, when the ban was lifted, it used to dominate the Downtown skyline. Today it maintains the original interior of mural ceilings, luxurious woods and refined detailing.

The "Triforium," an animated sculpture with a light show computer-keyed to music, outside the Los Angeles Mall - the Federal Courts building in the background.

Entrance to the Los Angeles Children's Museum, situated at the Los Angeles Mall, on Main Street.

Fountain with totem at the Los Angeles Mall - the Children's Museum is in the background.

Right behind the City Hall Tower, to the east, on the lower level of Main Street, you will find the **Los Angeles Mall** with its shops, restaurants, tropical plants, fountains and sculptures. At the northern end of the mall you can visit, on weekends, the **Los Angeles Children's Museum**, famous for its wonderful 'interactive' exhibits created for the joy of the little ones as well as their parents.
From Main Street walk back to First Street and going two blocks down to the east, enter **Little Tokyo**, the center of L.A.'s Japanese community. You should visit the **Japanese-American Cultural and Community Center**, where you can see a traditional Kabuki theater performance, a Japanese garden and the **Doizaki Gallery**, which exhibits works by Japanese and Japanese-American artists. There is also the **Japanese American National Museum**, illustrating the history of Japanese immigration to the U.S. Finally, walk through **Japanese Village Plaza**, which resembles a rural native village and offering a variety of fine shops and restaurants. Nearby you will find the **TOCA** (Temporary Contemporary), an enormous art exhibition auxiliary to the MOCA, obtained from a refurbished warehouse.

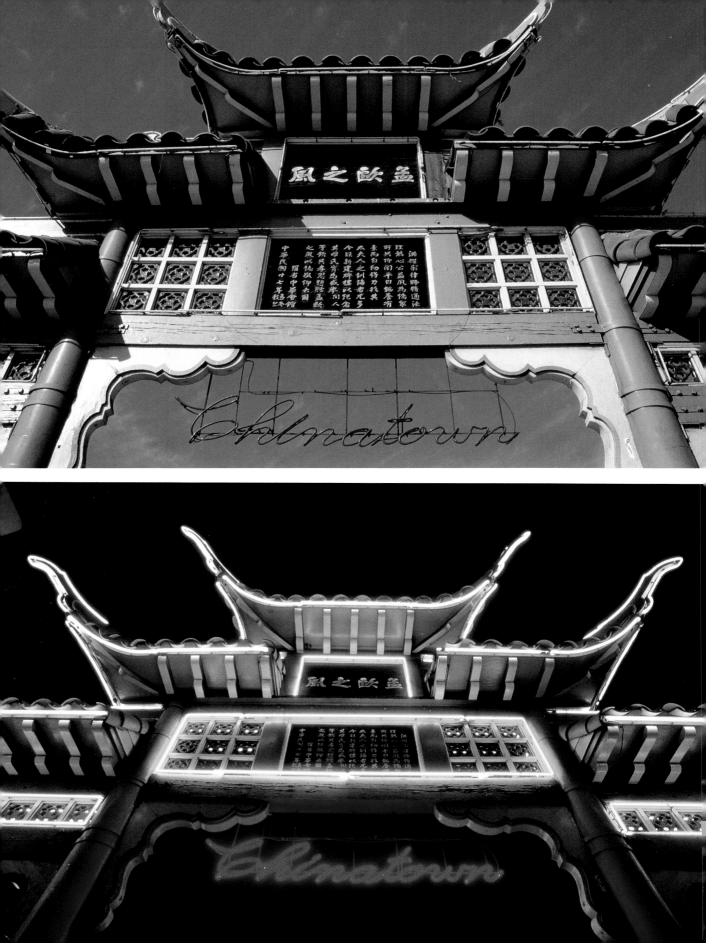

Two views of the entrance to Mandarin Plaza *in Chinatown.*
Bottom left: *Night view of the gate welcoming visitors to*
Mandarin Plaza.

Main entrance to the heart of the New Chinatown - *the mall*
called Mandarin Plaza.

CHINATOWN

If you wish to continue your tour through the fascinating cultural diversity of Downtown, you have to go to **Chinatown**, situated at its northern edge, right across from the 101 Freeway. Here the colorful, ornate architecture is in sharp contrast to the modern skyscrapers of the business district. Although a bit smaller than the equivalent in San Francisco, and by now pretty different from the original Chinatown which inspired Roman Polanski's classic film of the same name, the area offers an example of a vibrant ethnic community well-known for its distinctive restaurants, pastry-shops and produce markets. You can go on Sunday morning and experience 'dim sum' (Chinese brunch) at one of the many local eateries, then walk around the odd collections of shops at **Mandarin Plaza**, whose traditional **gate** welcomes visitors from all over the world. Many of the shops are filled with embroidered kimonos, Chinese slippers, Oriental toys, china and jewelry. Other more upscale establishments specialize in inlaid furniture, Asian art and fine silks. If you happen to be in Los Angeles during the month of January, you want to be in Chinatown for the **Chinese New Year Celebration** and enjoy the **Golden Dragon Parade**, along with arts and crafts, music and special foods.

EL PUEBLO - UNION STATION

Now be ready for another 'time travel', but this time more than 200 years in the past! Within walking distance from Chinatown, to the east, you will encounter the **El Pueblo de Los Angeles Historic Park** (also known simply as **El Pueblo**), site of the city's original nucleus. It was near here that in 1781, Felipe de Neve, the Spanish Governor, founded the minuscule town, then counting only 11 families and later to be known as Los Angeles. You can book a free walking tour of this most interesting district by going to the Docent Office on Paseo de la

View of Olvera Street, *in* El Pueblo de Los Angeles Historic Park, *the birth place of the city in 1781, when Alta California, along with Mexico, was still part of the Spanish Empire.*

Testimony of the Spanish and Mexican heritage displayed in the stall of Olvera Street.

Plaza. You can somewhat relive the atmosphere of early L.A., when cattle-raising 'señors' were bringing their families from distant ranches to Downtown for weekend fiestas, by going through the cobblestoned **Olvera Street**. Here, the first settlers established a homestead, **Avila Adobe**, which still exists. Built in 1818, this is L.A.'s oldest house. Go inside and discover what the furnishings of an early Californian family looked like. Olvera Street is an island for pedestrians only, lined with colorful stalls selling authentic Mexican products and with excellent restaurants. The narrow street leads to the **Old**

Plaza, characterized by its circular lacy wrought-iron bandstand. Here you can visit the **Old Plaza Roman Catholic Church**, dating from 1822, the oldest in the city, and the first **Firehouse** ever built in Los Angeles.

Walking east of El Pueblo to Alameda Street, you will arrive at **Union Station**. The imposing white mission-style structure dates back to 1939 - the last grand train station to be built in the United States before the explosion of air-travelling. From Union Station go back to Pershing Square riding the brand new Red Line subway.

Replica of the bell of the church in Dolores, birthplace of the Mexican Independence.

Tiled mural commemorating the beginning of the Mexican War of Independence .
Bottom right: *Another view of* El Pueblo de Los Angeles - the Mexican Cultural Institute.

On page 30: *main entrance to the renovated* Mission-style Union Station, *dating back to 1939 and Los Angeles' train connection to the rest of the country.*

On page 31: *view of the Downtown skyscrapers with the* Westin Bonaventure Hotel *in the background.*

Los Angeles County
Museum of Art

The Pavilion for Japanese Art *at the* Los Angeles County Museum of Art.

Northbound view of the business district in Downtown Los Angeles.

Life-size sculpture of a prehistoric mammoth at La Brea Tar Pits.

The main entrance to the Los Angeles County Museum of Art.

TO THE L.A. COUNTY MUSEUM OF ART THROUGH WILSHIRE

From Downtown you can start your exploration of Greater Los Angeles by taking **Wilshire Boulevard**, in many ways the stretched, L.A. version of New York's Fifth Avenue or Paris' Champs-Elysees. Between Highland and Fairfax Avenue you will go through the so-called **Miracle Mile**, one of the city's first suburban shopping developments, constructed by realtors in the 1930s to attract motorists.

Almost at the end of Miracle Mile, you will notice a park with a lake, from which a life-like mammoth emerges. Welcome to the **Hancock Park Complex and La Brea Tar Pits**! Here you have the richest fossil site inherited from the Ice-Age. Some 40,000 years ago the pits began attracting an incredible variety of prehistoric animals to water - only to be trapped forever. In 1906, an excavation and classification of the fossils was started and in the years to follow more than one and a half million specimens were dug up, mostly giant ones such as mastodons (ancestors of the elephants) and even

camels, but also many distant relatives of today's birds, lizards, bears and rodents. For a richer understanding of this unique treasure you should visit the **George C.Page La Brea Discoveries Museums**, offering the reconstructed skeletons of the animals, as well as documentaries and slides. In the same area you will find the **Los Angeles County Museum of Art (LACMA)**, a complex of four buildings surrounding a vast central atrium. This is certainly one of the nation's top museums and certainly the most important in the west. The **Ahmanson Building** houses, in addition to 19th- and 20th century European paintings, one of the world's largest collections of pre-Columbian, Tibetan, Indian, Nepalese and Islamic art. The more recent **Robert O. Anderson Building** features 20th century art along with special exhibits. The latest addition to the complex is the **Pavilion for Japanese Art**, displaying the internationally known Shin'enkan collection of Japanese paintings.

33

The moving traffic on the freeways becomes an incessant stream of light, right into a beautiful Southern California sunset.

Automobiles have become the fuel which runs through the city arteries known as freeways - a view of the 110 Harbor Freeway connecting Pasadena with San Pedro harbor and passing through Downtown.

Aerial view of two overpasses on the Harbor Freeway in Downtown Los Angeles.

Following pages: commercial buildings and residences alike seem small in comparison to the freeways in this spectacular view of the intersection between the 10 and the 110 Freeways, just south of Downtown.

L.A. FREEWAYS

"In L.A., they say, you are what you drive." In few other cities around the world is having a car, and preferably a good one is so important. An average of 8 million cars and commercial vehicles travel throughout the Greater Los Angeles Basin on a normal day. Hence the extreme importance of an efficient and fast way to cover the many miles often separating the various communities this megalopolis is made of. The L.A. freeway system is an impressive modern monument to such a need. But one warning: try and avoid being caught, in this otherwise very fast mode of transportation, at rush hour, when hundreds of thousands of commuters try to reach their work place or return home at the same time. Recently, in order to reduce traffic congestion and its ensuing pollution, a serious attempt has been made at changing the "One Man, One Car Philosophy." A series of incentives to car-pool have been introduced. And, great step towards an improved public transportation system is represented by the expansion of a new network of subways and commuter trains.

Von Kleinsmed building *on the University of Southern California (USC) campus.*

Sculpture of a Trojan, symbol of USC - administration buildings and the Bobard Auditorium *in the background.*

Home to two Olympiads and innumerable athletic competitions as well as artistic performances, the Los Angeles Memorial Coliseum, *inspired by Rome's Colosseum.*

USC AND THE COLISEUM

Directly south of Downtown at the corner of Jefferson Boulevard and Figueroa Street, lies the beautiful campus of the private **University of Southern California (USC)**, with its excellent galleries and art museums open to the public. The **Fisher Gallery's** impressive collection includes Dutch, Italian and American art from the 15th century to the present. The **Hancock Memorial Museum** contains artifacts from the Mexico City palace of Emperor Maximilian and Empress Carlotta. The **Helen Lindhurst Architecture Gallery**, on the second floor of Watt Hall, displays architectural exhibits. And talking about architecture, you cannot miss the **Doheny Library**, built in 1932, one of USC's most striking landmarks. The University is renown, amongst other things, for its **School of Cinema and Television** (director Steven Spielberg is one of its most famous alumni). The **USC Cinema Special Collection Library** exhibits scripts, movie stills and scrapbooks donated by past Hollywood celebrities such as Clark Gable, Fritz Lang and Fay Wray.

Continuing on Figueroa Street you will reach the 114-acre Exposition Park. Originally an agricultural fairground and horse-racing track, the area was converted to a public park at the end of last century. Today it offers a rose garden, museums such as the **California Museum of Science and Industry**, the **Afro-American Museum** and the **Natural History Museum** and sports arenas. Amongst the latter the **Los Angeles Memorial Coliseum** deserves particular mention. Modeled after Rome's Colosseum, the huge structure was built in 1928, in honor of America's World War I veterans. The Coliseum was home to both the 1932 Olympic Games and the 1984 Summer Olympic track and field events. Today, it's home to the Los Angeles Raiders and to the USC Trojans football teams. It also hosts motorcycle racing, rodeos and other sporting events.

The nearby **Los Angeles Sports Arena** is a smaller facility, home to the L.A. Clippers and USC Trojans basketball teams.

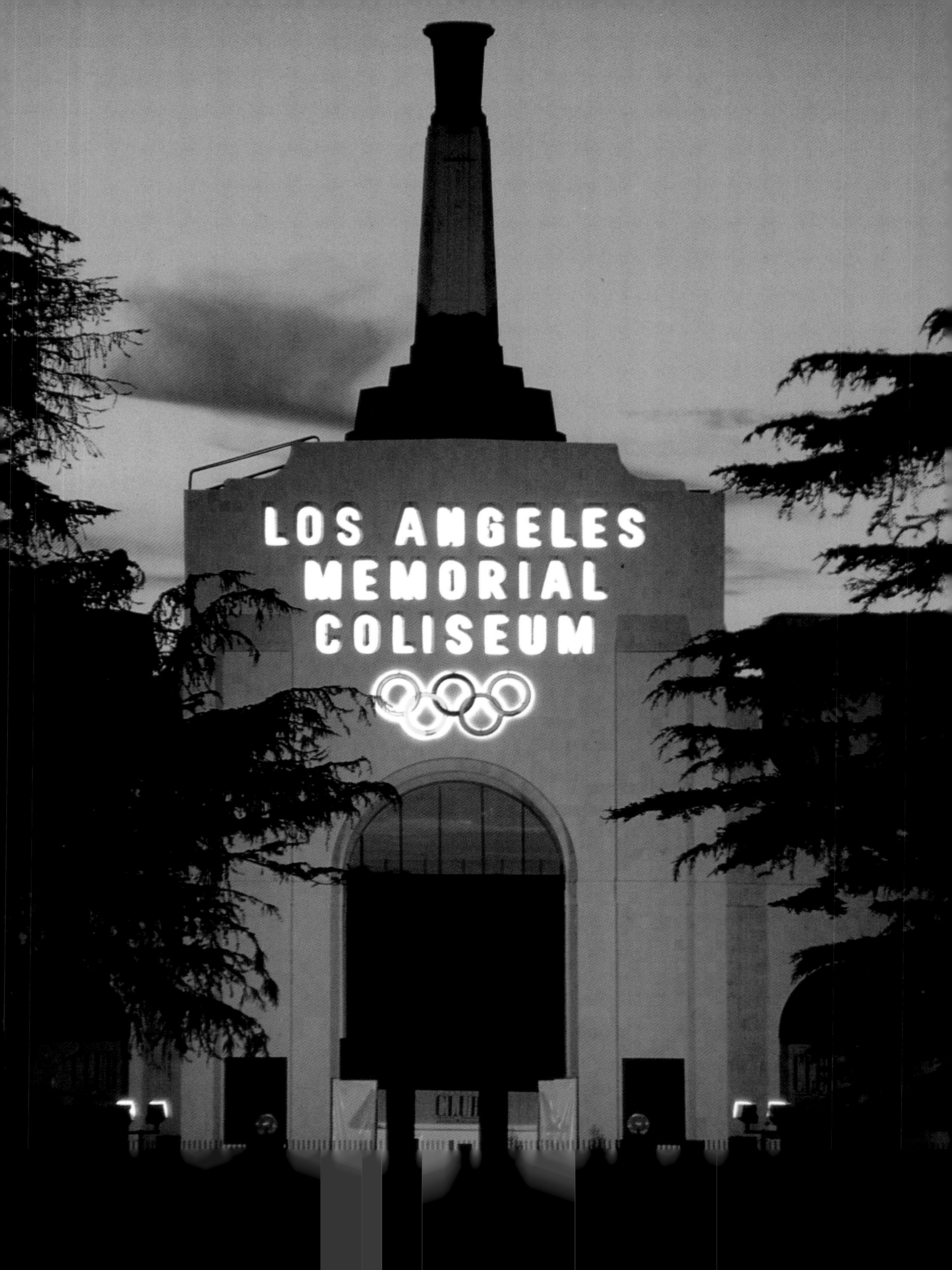
LOS ANGELES
MEMORIAL
COLISEUM

HOLLYWOOD

Symbol of stardom dreams, the world-famous Hollywood sign stands at the top of the Hollywood Hills, overlooking the city. Originally the sign used to say "Hollywoodland," and it served as advertising for real estate development on the hills. Then the "land" part fell off and the sign, in its present form, was kept as a landmark.

A night view of Downtown from the Hollywood Hills.

Following pages: the ocean of streets and houses of Los Angeles as it appears at night from the vantage point of the Hollywood Hills. A sight made familiar by the many films shot in this city.

HOLLYWOOD BOULEVARD

Hollywood, Hollywood!! All over the world the name of what used to be, up to the beginning of this century a tiny farming's community, evokes legendary wonders. The name Hollywood has by now a magic resonance. Hollywood has become synonymous with the world of movies - not just the making of them, but the whole aura surrounding them - most especially the life of the stars, the directors and the producers.
That is why millions of people every year come to Los Angeles. For many of them the main attraction does remain Hollywood, as if they could, almost by osmosis, become part of this world or, if not, take a much closer look at it. Yet one thing has to be realized immediately. During the Golden Era of the Hollywood system (the '20s, '30s and the '40s) most of the famous studios were spread out outside the strict boundaries of Hollywood. The only true exception was and still is Paramount Studios.

And many of the crucial decisions about the course of the movie industry take place in the mansions in Beverly Hills and Bel Air, maybe by a pool or at a party, away from the busy streets of Hollywood proper.
A tour of Hollywood can start from the world-famous **Grauman's (now Mann's) Chinese Theatre** located at 6925 Hollywood Boulevard. This was Sid Grauman's movie palace salute to the King Tut craze of the 1920s. For the facade he even imported the pillars of a Chinese temple. In the silent screen era, stars arrived here in furs and tails for movie premieres. Some premieres are still held today at the Chinese Theater, but clearly not with the same pomp and ostentation as in the old days. In front of the theater lobby (a reminder of the splendor that once was Hollywood) you can see the much talked about hand and footprints left by many screen celebrities. Some of them went beyond a simple

Hollywood Boulevard *is flanked by majestic palm trees and modern buildings.*

Main entrance to the famous Mann's Chinese Theater *on Hollywood Boulevard.*

The floor at the entrance to the Chinese Theater has been immortalized by the hand and shoe imprints of Hollywood's most famous stars through the years.

imprint in the cement. John Barrymore, for instance, left an impression of his profile, William S. Hart of his gun, and Gene Autry of the hoof prints of Champ, his horse. More recently directors Steven Spielberg and George Lucas left sneaker prints. Once you are there, do feel free to try and match your feet and hands with those of the stars imbedded in the cement.

Right across from the Chinese Theater and a bit down east, you can admire another monument to the Golden Era of cinema: **Mann's Egyptian Theatre**, Hollywood's first movie palace. Built in 1922 and now under restoration, it was the setting for spectacular movie premieres, with studio extras robed as Egyptian guards and all usherettes looking like potential Cleopatras. Also worth noting is the nearby **El Capitan** (1926), featuring a Spanish baroque exterior and an Art Deco interior. The site of Citizen

A myriad of neon signs adorn the stores on Hollywood Boulevard.

The newest development on Hollywood Boulevard, next to the Chinese Theater: a multiplex movie theater complex called the Hollywood Galaxy.

The Tyrannosaurus rex atop "Ripley's Believe It or Not! Odditorium" threatens pedestrians walking along Hollywood Boulevard at the intersection with Highland.

The world-known Walk of Fame on the sidewalks of Hollywood Boulevard.

You cannot escape the Hollywood sign, in all its forms!

The unique shape of the Capitol Records Building in Hollywood: a stack of records with a needle on top, another symbol of L.A. as Entertainment Capital of the World. In the foreground a mural celebrating legendary Nat King Cole.

Kane's world premiere in 1941, it is today a regular movie theater and a showplace for Walt Disney's world premieres.

One block east of the Chinese Theatre, right after **Highland Avenue**, is Spoony Singh's **Hollywood Wax Museum**, a further celebration of the Dream Factory. Spoony bought the museum more than thirty years ago, when it was in a state of total disarray. Just to give a couple of examples, Shirley Temple's head had shrunk dramatically, while Mickey Rooney's arms had fallen off. The ''new'' Wax Museum is in perfect order and contains 185 figures. The only problem, at least for a while, was that guests continually stole Raquel Welch's bras, until the management decided to let her be altogether braless. Although you can find the very publicized tableaux of John F. Kennedy at the lectern, of Leonardo Da Vinci's Last Supper and of Queen Victoria and Martin Luther King here, the majority of wax figures portray movie stars or celebrities from the entertainment world. You don't want to miss the most famous tableau, the one representing Marilyn Monroe in her unforgettable dress-blowing scene from *The Seven-Year Itch*. A new attraction is the **Movie Awards Theatre,** presenting a film that covers more than half a century of Academy Award winners and presentations. In the sound track you will recognize the songs that were voted best each year. As you stroll along either side of Hollywood Boulevard you will inevitably notice the succession of bronze medallions with the name of stars and leading character actors inserted in the pavement. You have just stepped on the **Walk of Fame**. The name of personalities - and not just the screen legends - are symbolized in his or her medium, be it film, radio, music or television. Each time a new star-shaped medallion is embedded, a little ceremony with the honoree, attracting an army of reporters, paparazzi and TV cameras, is held on the sidewalk itself.

Murals adorn a few side streets on Hollywood Boulevard. This one in particular shows some of Hollywood most famous stars looking at us from the seats of a movie theater.

A political-psychedelic mural, reminding to us the ecological destruction and the contrast between rich and poor on Planet Earth.

Continuing eastward you will reach the much talked about corner of Hollywood and Vine. Although legendary, it is architecturally unimpressive. It remains famous in the collective memory and imagination for the number of stars who used to cross the intersection. Between Highland and Vine you can find a whole series of novelty and book shops, as well as many movie memorabilia and poster shops. If you walk a couple of blocks north of Vine you reach the **Capitol Records Building**, a unique architectural structure, shaped like a stack of records with a needle on top.

Movie buffs might want to go a few blocks south, to 6000 Santa Monica Boulevard (between Van Ness and Gower) in order to visit the **Hollywood Memorial Park Cemetery** and pay homage to the crypt of Valentino. Also Peter Lorrie, Douglas Fairbanks, Norma Talmadge, Tyrone Power and Marion Davies are buried here.

A bit further south, on Melrose Avenue and Valentino on weekdays visitors can enjoy a tour of **Paramount Studios**. In the same area there are smaller independent studios, film-development labs, and other auxiliary services, such as prop rental outlets related to the movie industry.

In the northern hills behind Hollywood you can find a beautiful area, called **Hollywoodland**, with a dam and a lake surrounded by many precious homes. This is the location of the world-famous **Hollywood sign.** In the '20s the sign, originally an advertising for real estate development, used to read '' Hollywoodland''.

West of Hollywoodland, on Cahuenga, you can take Mulholland Drive, a unique scenic road from which you can simultaneously see both the Los Angeles Basin and the San Fernando Valley. From here you can practically reach the sea at Topanga Canyon, north of Malibu.

The white tower advertising the Farmers Market, *one of the main attractions in the* Fairfax *district.*

One of the many colorful displays of fresh fruit at the Farmers Market.

WEST HOLLYWOOD AND THE FARMERS MARKET

Traveling south-west of the Chinese Theatre, you can reach **West Hollywood** along **Sunset Boulevard**. Immediately west of Crescent Heights you will find the legendary **Chateau Marmont**, one of Hollywood's oldest hotels, styled like a 17th century French castle. It is from here, on Sunset, that the famous **Strip** starts. The Strip is also well-known for its comedy clubs, avant-garde bookstores, outdoor bistros and fine restaurants, including **Le Dome, Spago** and **Nicky Blair**, where movie celebrities and power brokers tend to go when out to "do" lunch. The last part of the Strip is world-famous for its rock clubs such as the **Roxy**, the **Whiskey** and the **Rainbow Bar & Grill**. Just before reaching the Strip you can instead take **Fairfax Avenue**, heart of L.A.'s Jewish community, and go down south to Third Street. Here is the **Farmers Market**, with its open-air vegetable and fruit stalls, its restaurants offering a rich variety of cuisines and its souvenir shops.

MELROSE AVENUE

From Fairfax, a bit north of the Farmer's Market you can take **Melrose Avenue.** It is advisable to park your car and stroll up and down this novel shopping district which has often been compared to London's Kings Road. Located in the middle of an Orthodox Jewish neighborhood, this eclectic street is the home of the hip and trendy. The merchandise includes everything from funky antiques to sophisticated clothing to new wave to high-tech furnishings and collector's comic books. Even if you are not in the mood to buy anything, the fun remains in admiring the creativity which goes into the storefronts and window displays. At the western end of Melrose, you might want to go and visit the **Pacific Design Center**, also known locally as the "Blue Whale" because of its size and color. Opened in 1975 as a place where design industry professionals could buy and sell their wares, today the PDC has opened its doors to non-professionals and is full of shops specializing in interior furnishings.

Shops of any kind and original window displays can be found on trendy Melrose Avenue.

Outside Johnny Rockets, on Melrose Avenue. Johnny Rockets is a 1950s style hamburger, fries, malts and pies eatery. It has become a chain, and another identical establishment can be found in downtown Beverly Hills.

An aerial view of the Griffith Observatory *in Griffith Park, the largest urban wilderness area in the United States.*

A closer look at the Griffith Observatory, *featuring planetarium and laserium shows.*

Monument in the square next to the Observatory, celebrating the great names in the history of astronomy. It was here that the last dramatic scene of the classic film Rebels Without a Cause, with James Dean was shot.

GRIFFITH PARK AND OBSERVATORY

North of Hollywood Boulevard, east of the Hollywood sign, you can find the splendid natural haven called **Griffith Park**. With 4000 acres of sage and manzanilla covered hills and 53 miles of hiking and equestrian trails, this is the largest urban wilderness area in the United States. Once part of Rancho Los Feliz, the park was named after its former owner, the notorious Colonel Griffith J. Griffith, who spent a year in prison for attempting to murder his wife. Griffith gave the land to the city of Los Angeles in 1896. Scandalized by Griffith's behavior, city leaders refused to accept the money Griffith offered to construct an observatory, until after his death in 1898.

You can reach the **Griffith Observatory and Planetarium** from the **Vermont Avenue** entrance, passing through the **Greek Theatre** - a picturesque open-air amphitheater offering ballets, light operas and rock, country western and jazz concerts. The Griffith Observatory features a 650-seat **planetarium theater**, where **astronomy shows** are held daily. **Laserium shows**, featuring a dazzling combination of light and music under the planetarium stars, are offered nightly. The **Hall of Science** features a collection of meteorites and geological specimens, and exhibits explaining physics principles and scientific equipment. The Observatory has been made famous by the classic '50s film *Rebel without a Cause*, with James Dean. A plaque with the profile of the young movie legend can be found in front of the Observatory, to commemorate the shooting of the film in and outside the building.

In addition to the landmark observatory, the park offers, in close vicinity to each other, attractions such as the **Los Angeles Zoo**, displaying more than 2000 animals in areas which simulate natural habitats; the **Gene Autry Western Heritage Museum**, a splendid introduction to the Wild West, and the **Travel Town Transportation Museum**, displaying locomotives, airplanes, trolleys and trains.

Two views of the Hollywood Bowl, site of many wonderful "concerts under the stars," one of the city's main attractions in the summer months - the Hollywood Hills in the background.

HOLLYWOOD BOWL

Nestled in the Hollywood foothills, just to the west of the sign is the **Hollywood Bowl**, summer home of the Los Angeles Philharmonic Orchestra since 1922, and also home to the Hollywood Bowl Orchestra. Top-name performers such as Cleo Laine and Sting have drawn sellout crowds here. The most popular concerts each season are the Fourth of July Fireworks Family Picnic Concert and the two-day Tchaikovsky Spectacular with cannon shots, fireworks, and a military band. Other presentations include numerous opera and pop concerts, the traditional Easter Sunrise Service, and the "Open House at the Bowl" children's festival. The L.A. Philharmonic season runs from July through September. Recently the Playboy Jazz Festival has held its rich program in this natural setting amphitheater. Most of the performances take place in the evening, under the stars, and picnicking on the grounds before a concert is one of the most exquisite summer pleasures in L.A.

A fire explodes in a Far Western town - right in front of your eyes. Not to worry. This 'controlled' piece of fiction can be enjoyed at the Wild, Wild, Wild West Stunt Show, one of the many forms of entertainment for the visitors of "movie worlds", all part of the Universal City Studios Tour.

UNIVERSAL CITY STUDIOS

On the hills between Hollywood and the San Fernando Valley, a few minutes from the intersection of Highland and Hollywood Boulevard, there is one of L.A.'s biggest year-round attractions: **Universal City Studios**. This is the largest studio in the world, with 561 separate buildings sprawling over 420 acres of mountain terrain and valley.

It is difficult to believe that up to World War I this used to be a mere chicken-ranch! A lot has surely changed since Carl Laemmle founded the studio in 1915. In the '30s Universal became famous for its thrillers and horror films, starting with the classic Frankenstein. Let us not forget that British director Alfred Hitchcock found a "home" at Universal. More recently the studio is associated with blockbusters such as *Jaws*, *E.T.*, *Conan the Barbarian*, and, last but not least, *Jurassic Park*.

Starting at the **Visitors Entertainment Center**, you can take a **guided tour** aboard one of the brightly colored trams. Often your tour guide is an aspiring actor or actress. The tour takes you through the entire studio. The major attractions are the spectacular re-enactments of some of Universal's most recent hits. The **Back to the Future Ride** allows you to travel through time, back to the Ice-Age and forward to the year 2015. In the **Backdraft 'show'** you are engulfed in a firestorm of special effects, even a river of fire. You can participate in the **E.T. Adventure** and help the most famous extra-terrestrial in movie history to save his planet. You can actually live through an 8.3 tremor in the **Earthquake Ride**. One of earliest shows is called **Kongfrontation**, where you meet King Kong, the greatest monster in movie history. You can meet another well - known monster in the **Jaws Ride**. Yet another very interesting part is a guided tour through "**movie worlds**" - you can pass from Six

Points Texas, a western town with six intersecting streets, to a European Street, to a Colonial Street (Smalltown, U.S.A.) and a New York Street. This is just a sample of the sets you can visit to get a "behind the scenes" idea of how movie-making works. Many others are open to the general public, including those utilized for current TV shows such as *Murder She Wrote*, *Coach*, *Major Dad*, *Northern Exposure* and *Seaquest* . In **The Magic of Alfred Hitchcock**, you can find out more about the secrets of the famous *Psycho* shower scene. For those who love action there is **The Wild, Wild, Wild West Stunt Show**, where one can enjoy a series of amazing antics by some of the best stunt people in the film business.

Equally thrilling is **The Adventures of Conan**, a magic show of sword fights, lasers and fireballs, inspired by another Universal blockbuster, *Conan the Barbarian* . If you are a 'trekkie', or simply a fan of *Star Trek*, you cannot miss **Star Trek Adventure**, allowing you to be aboard the Starship Enterprise and "boldly go where no one has gone before." Children are regularly charmed by **An American Tail Show**, based on the famous Universal cartoon and can also enjoy the giant props of **Fievel's Playland**. Another great attraction for those visiting the Universal Studios is the opportunity to witness the actual production of a movie and to meet the stars. Suddenly, during your tour, they might ask you to be "Quiet on the set," and if you are lucky you might even go back home with your favorite star's autograph.

Universal City has been rightly defined "the Entertainment Capital of the Entertainment Capital," and it surely represents a major competition for Disneyland. Beyond the magic of the tour and the shows, the visitor can now also stroll through the recently built **Universal CityWalk**, a "futuristic village" within the city, with its lively concentration of restaurants, shops and street performers.

At the Wild, Wild Wild West Stunt show, those who love action can witness this kind of brawl amongst some of the best stunt people in the movie business.

An aerial view of the Mormon Temple *(in the foreground). In the background the quaint 'village' of Westwood and behind it the* UCLA *campus and the hills of the super-residential area known as* Bel Air.
Royce Hall *on the UCLA campus, one of the most important universities in California.*

WESTWOOD - UCLA AND THE MORMON TEMPLE

Another little "city within the city" is **Westwood**, a quaint community practically half way between Hollywood and the ocean. This exciting area not only includes the **University of California at Los Angeles (UCLA)**, but also the "village" itself, with its variety of movie theaters, bookstores and restaurants. The 411-acre UCLA campus is just north of the village and features museums, theaters, magnificent architecture and beautifully landscaped grounds. Do not miss the Franklin D. Murphy Sculpture Garden, containing more than 70 works by masters such as Rodin, Matisse, Moore and Miró. South of the village, a new addition to L.A.'s cultural life is the recently established **Armand Hammer Museum of Art**, legacy of the late oil tycoon. And further south you can admire a unique building: the **Mormon Temple**, with its vast, picture-perfect lawn. At the Visitors Center you can watch a movie about the interior of the temple which is otherwise closed to the general public.

Aerial view of Beverly Hills. The mansions with their manicured lawns and pools are the inevitable part of a landscape made famous by many films and TV series.

Extra-tall palm-trees adorn the entrance to the legendary Beverly Hills Hotel, at the heart of Beverly Hills' residential area.

A closer detail of the Beverly Hills Hotel. The Polo Lounge is a customary meeting place for the powerful wheeler-dealers in the entertainment community.

BEVERLY HILLS

Although not necessarily or strictly related to the world of movies, **Beverly Hills**, like Hollywood, contains a special resonance throughout the world, even for those who simply hear or say its name. This autonomous municipality, completely encircled by Los Angeles, has become synonymous with a luxurious life-style which is not just typical of motion-picture stars, though they can be described as its original 'colonizers'. It was in 1919 that silent-screen stars Mary Pickford and Douglas Fairbanks moved to this area and built their famous estate, Pickfair, hence starting a migration of movie celebrities that has never stopped. Located immediately west of Hollywood, Beverly Hills is mostly flat, with its northern section occupying the foothills of the Santa Monica mountain range. In 1914, when it was created, it contained only 675 registered voters. In the '20s it became a "boom town" and has now become a population of more than 35,000 people. The **Civic Center** and **City Hall**, built in 1932, are classic examples of the city's Spanish Renaissance architecture. You might also want to drive around the residential area north of Santa Monica Boulevard and just enjoy the amazing variety of beautiful houses and mansions. An important stop is the recently renovated **Beverly Hills Hotel**, with its **Polo Lounge**, where exclusive wheeling and dealing within the entertainment business traditionally occurs.

Aerial view of Century City.
To the right, at the top, the structures of the 20th Century Fox Studios. *In the foreground is* Santa Monica Boulevard. *Right behind Century City, a line of tall buildings indicates* Wilshire Boulevard, *stretching all the way to the skyscrapers of Downtown at the horizon.*

A closer look at Century City. Avenue of the Stars *crosses* Olympic Boulevard *with an overpass. In the background to the right the* Golden Traingle *of downtown Beverly Hills. Many entertainment companies and law firms have their offices in the skyscrapers of Century City. Also former president Ronald Reagan has his office here.*

Beverly Hills has an undeniable reputation as a "shopper's paradise". But even if you don't feel like shopping, you might simply enjoy strolling around the so-called "**Golden Triangle**" district, bordered by Little Santa Monica, Crescent Drive and Wilshire Boulevard. You cannot miss **Rodeo Drive**, cutting through the center of the triangle and world-famous for its collection of glossy high-fashion boutiques. A recent development is **Two Rodeo Drive**, probably one of the most expensive shopping complexes ever built - its original cost was $130 million. You can visit its exclusive boutiques and salons in a European-style setting of cobblestone streets, elegant steps and an Italianate piazza. If shopping for high-fashion clothes or jewelry is not your primary interest, do not forget that each avenue of the Golden Triangle abounds with exquisite art galleries, antique shops and quaint restaurants.

CENTURY CITY

Adjacent to Beverly Hills, to the west, is **Century City**, the home of **Twentieth Century Fox Studios** and a large business center. Originally part of the studio's enormous backlot, Century City is today the site of a **Shopping Center** and **Marketplace**, featuring 140 stores, an international food court and a 14-screen movie theater.

A very interesting addition to this area is the Simon Wiesenthal Center's new **Museum of Tolerance**, on Pico Boulevard, offering an in-depth look at racism and prejudice in the modern world.

Interactive and hands-on exhibits encourage visitors to see the world through other people's eyes as they explore 20th century genocide, war and oppression, including the Holocaust.

A view of the pier and the beach in 'downtown' Malibu.

MALIBU

Twenty-five miles from the Los Angeles Civic Center, along the Pacific Coast Highway north of Santa Monica, lies the world-famous community (or 'colony' as it is called) of **Malibu.** Its name is derived from the Chumash Indian word "Umalibo," once a native settlement. Part of a vast Spanish ranch in the early 19th century, it was bought during the "Panic of 1857" by a shrewd Irishman for 10 cents an acre. Later on it was seen by Yankee Frederick Hastings Rindge, who purchased it in 1887, as a potential "American Riviera." Rindge, and later on his wife, tried to keep Malibu in its pristine state. But in 1927, the first movie stars arrived. Anna

Q. Nillsson was followed by Clara Bow and John Gilbert, to mention a few, and the 'wild' parties of the Roaring '20s kept more than one gossip columnist busy. In 1929, after a long legal battle between California and Mrs. Rindge, the Pacific Coast Highway (back then called Roosevelt Highway) was inaugurated and extensive development ensued. Nevertheless, even today, this residential area does not offer the offensive spectacle of high-rise buildings to be witnessed in no few parts of the French, Italian or Spanish Rivieras.
Today, the **Malibu Beach Colony**, is still the home of many stars and one could jokingly describe it as a

"Beverly Hills by-the-sea," without the shopping. You might want to stroll along the beach, take a swim or simply enjoy some seafood in the **Malibu Pier** area. And of course, whether you are ready to join them or not, you cannot miss the regular antics of the **surfers** riding the ocean waves, even in the winter, when they wear wetsuits. North of the Malibu Pier area, on the hills above the sea, you can go and visit **Pepperdine University** and enjoy the scenic view from its modern campus. If you keep driving north along the coast, you will encounter a series of vast sand beaches, starting with the beautiful **Zuma Beach.** Or if you like hiking you might want to explore the many trails on the mountains behind the ocean.

The quaint architecture of the Malibu Beach Inn.

One of the many beaches in Malibu.

THE J. PAUL GETTY MUSEUM

If you take Sunset Boulevard from Beverly Hills (the Beverly Hills Hotel might be a very good starting point), and go west, you will be first bordering the super-residential area known as **Bel Air** on the hills to the north, and the **UCLA Campus** to the south. After crossing the 405 Freeway you will enter the quaint neighborhood of **Brentwood**. It was here that Marilyn Monroe spent the last period of her life (her house is at 12305 5th Helena Drive).

After Brentwood, Sunset Boulevard continues its winding all the way to the ocean through the residential area of **Pacific Palisades**. Once you have reached the **Pacific Coast Highway**, you can go north for a mile and stop at the magnificent **J. Paul Getty Museum**. Also dubbed "Pompeii-by-the-Pacific," the museum is a spectacular reconstruction of a Roman villa with interior and exterior gardens - to be more specific, the Villa dei Papiri, which was buried in volcanic mud during the eruption of Mount Vesuvius in A.D. 779.

The J. Paul Getty Museum (inaugurated in 1974) is one of seven programs of the J.Paul Getty Trust, a private operating foundation devoted to the visual arts. The Museum houses permanent collections of Greek and Roman antiquities, pre-twentieth-century European paintings (amongst which is the only documented painting in the country by Italian Renaissance master Masaccio), drawings, sculpture, illuminated manuscripts, decorative arts, and nineteenth- and twentieth-century European and American photographs.

The Museum's gardens include trees, flowers, shrubs, and herbs like those that might have been found growing two thousand years ago at the Villa dei Papiri. The bronze statues in the gardens are modern casts of statues unearthed during the 18th century explorations of the Villa (the originals are at Naples' Archaeological Museum).

An aerial view of the J.Paul Getty Museum *between Santa Monica and Malibu. The structure is a replica of the Roman Villa dei Papiri, originally covered by the ashes of the famous Mount Vesuvius eruption which destroyed Pompeii and Haerculanum.*

Entrance to the Santa Monica Pier *at sunset. The pier contains many attractions, amongst which include a carousel and bumper-cars. At the end of the pier anglers gather day and night to catch fish.*

SANTA MONICA

They say that if you ask the average L.A. resident which part of the city he or she would most like to live in, nine times out of 10 the answer will be **Santa Monica**. And not surprisingly so. Located at the very beginning of the Pacific Coast Highway, between the ocean and the mountains, this community not only celebrates creativity and the arts, but is also known for being ecologically conscious. An integral part of its life-style is a definitively pedestrian-friendly downtown. Many people use their car as a method of transportation here, yet an equal number can be seen walking, bicycling, rollerskating and skateboarding.

A good way to start a tour of Santa Monica is by strolling along the scenic **Palisades Park**, which runs along the cliffs that overlook the ocean. At the southern end of this park, characterized by a succession of majestic palm-trees, you will find the recently renovated **Santa Monica Pier**, an historical landmark built in 1908. In those times a railway line used to connect Downtown Los Angeles with Santa Monica, and carried early tourists to the coast. Here the classic '70s film *The Sting* starring Paul Newman and Robert Redford, was shot. Along the boardwalk are old-fashioned kinds of amusements rarely found in cities these days: there is a beautiful carnival playground with a handcrafted carousel, bumper cars and arcades. You can also find a few little restaurants along the pier specializing mostly in seafood. A series of enlarged old black and white photos, part of an open-air exhibit, illustrate the history of Santa Monica, with a special attention to its beaches and boardwalk. At the very end of the pier you can easily go down to the vast beach for a walk. Or, if you feel more sportive, you can rent some roller-skates and race along the cement lane built purposely for this activity, as well as for bicycling. Inland from the Palisades Park you can reach the **Third Street Promenade**, open to pedestrian traffic only. Beginning at Broadway, the Promenade stretches north all the way to Wilshire Boulevard along Third Street. It is a lot of fun to walk along it any time of the day, but Friday and Saturday nights are particularly lively. Shops, cafes and restaurants are

Santa Monica beach. *The elevated wooden cabins are utilized by the ever-present beach-guards in the summer months.*

A just-before-nightfall view of Palisades Park, *overlooking the ocean, along* Ocean Boulevard *in Santa Monica.*

Volleyball players seem to have a great time next to the Santa Monica Pier *at dusk.*

A mural.

open late and it is very likely to find some street entertainment.

At the southern tip of the Promenade starts the **Santa Monica Place Mall**, a contemporary retail center with unique specialty shops and department stores reflecting, through their artsy, individual style, the creative attitude of the community.

The whole urban area by the ocean offers an incredible variety of restaurants, pubs, cafes, new and old-fashioned hotels and movie-theaters, all very easy to reach without ever using your car - a fairly unusual feature in Los Angeles, as you might have discovered by now!

South of this area you might wish to explore **Main Street**, stretching several blocks between Pico Boulevard and Marine. Although the shopping district and the surrounding residential

neighborhood has gone through an impressive revitalization in the last five years, signs of the past do coexist along with modern trends. Art galleries and antique shops can be found side by side with fine restaurants. Out on the street, on the walls, you can admire a series of decorative graphic murals. Another attractive shopping area is **Montana Avenue**, located between 26th Street and Ocean Avenue, closer to the mountains. Here you might feel you are walking along a quaint downtown street in small-town U.S.A.

At 2772 Donald Douglas Loop North, at the tiny tourist-oriented **Santa Monica Airport**, the **Museum of Flying** allows you to explore the history of flight. Amongst the most exciting attractions do not miss a high-tech motor simulator.

The Palisades Park.

Aerial view of Santa Monica, *with its beach and pier. The Santa Monica Pier, built in 1908, is the oldest pleasure pier still in operation on the West Coast. In the background, along the coast, the beach community of Malibu.*

The Santa Monica Pier *with its restaurants.*

A detail of the Santa Monica Pier *with its restaurants specializing in seafood.*

A view of the boardwalk in Venice Beach, with its open-air body building facility. It is in this community that Arnold Schwarzenegger started his career as body-builder, before becoming a multimillion dollar movie star.

Body-builders showing their muscles at Venice Beach. Roller-skaters, bicyclers, street vendors and musicians complete the crowd to be seen, especially on weekends, along the boardwalk.

VENICE BEACH

To the south of Santa Monica, driving along Ocean Avenue you can reach **Venice Beach**. This community has gone through a series of changes since the beginning of the century when visionary developer Abboy Kinney founded it with the intention of recreating its Italian namesake on the shores of the Pacific Ocean. Kinney went as far as building canals, one lane-bridges and importing gondolas. The St.Mark's, an Italian-style rococo hotel was born, while silent-screen star Mae Murray built a Venetian-style palazzo. A period of decay followed the discovery of oil, as derricks began substituting quaint residences. In the '50s Venice became a pole of attraction for the beatniks, followed by the hippies in the '60s. Recently the area has been enjoying a renaissance . Trendy art galleries and restaurants can be found, and it is chic again to live here. Especially on weekends, you can enjoy the lively **boardwalk** with its crowds of street vendors, body-builders and roller-skaters.

Undisturbed pelicans frequent the Fishermen's Village waterfront in Marina del Rey.

The 60-feet tall lighthouse in Marina del Rey's Fishermen's Village.

MARINA DEL REY

Bordering Venice to the south, you can visit the recently developed **Marina del Rey**. Here lies the largest small craft harbor in the world, a totally man-made creation, home to more than 6,000 boats of every kind, from yachts to schooners to sampans. Tours are regularly offered, or you can independently rent a boat and cruise around. During Christmas holidays you might want to enjoy a night-time parade displaying many of the marina's boats lighted and decorated for the occasion. On the Fourth of July, another attraction can be found in the impressive fireworks extravaganza. Beside the waterside **Restaurant Row**, with its array of different cuisines, the Old English style **Fisherman's Village** welcomes you on Fiji Way. The latter contains 40 specialty shops and restaurants lined along the cobblestoned walk by the waterfront. At the center of this area is a quaint 60-foot lighthouse. Free jazz concerts are featured on Sunday afternoons.

The Theme Building, *part of the $50 million Jet Age Terminal Construction Project begun in 1960, at LAX International Airport. The futuristic structure, with its restaurant and Observation Deck, displays two supporting arches with a steel core - it was the first time such type of design was used.*

Maritime theme of whales and dolphins in giant mural by the Venice Beach boardwalk.

The Korean Friendship Bell, *situated on a beautiful knoll overlooking the ocean in San Pedro. The giant bell is a gift to the United States by South Korea in occasion of the Bicentennial Celebration of 1976.*

LAX

Located twelve miles south of Downtown, lies the **Los Angeles International Airport**, also known in its short form as **LAX**. In 1926 the City of Los Angeles considered establishing a municipal airport on a ranch area by the water, just south of present day Marina del Rey. The earliest facility, opened in 1928 and called Mines Field, had no buildings and just dirt strips for runways, but in September of that year the National Air Races were held, in front of 200,000 spectators. It was here that the Graf Zeppelin landed in 1929, after a trans-pacific flight from Japan. When Vice President Lyndon B. Johnson dedicated the new Jet Age Central Terminal in 1961, commercial jet service was at its very beginnings. A further $700 million investment (the largest ever undertaken by a major airport) was necessary to adapt LAX to the revolutionary changes in air transportation. The transformation was completed by 1986. Today the Los Angeles International Airport, serving more than 85 major airlines and an annual traffic of over 5.6 million passengers, is the third largest airport in the world and certainly one of the most modern. It has a convenient U-shaped dual-level drive (the top level for departures, the lower one for arrivals), connecting each separate airline terminal. Each carrier has a specific Ticketing Building (also containing baggage check-in and claim facilities) connected by a long corridor to a satellite building that houses the aircraft gates. At the center of the U-shaped World Way loop are the parking facilities, the Airport Control Tower and the **Theme Building**. The latter is an interesting piece of architecture and deserves a visit. Part of the Jet Age Terminal Construction Project begun in 1960, it displays two futuristic concrete arches with a core steel support, the first of this type ever utilized. The theme building houses a gourmet restaurant and an **Observation Deck**, both offering a 360 degree panoramic view of LAX.

SAN PEDRO - LONG BEACH

Nestled on the slopes of the magnificent **Palos Verdes Peninsula** and still part of the city, the community of **San Pedro** looks southward across the sea to **Santa Catalina Island**. San Pedro's history goes back to 1542, when explorer-conquistador Juan Rodriguez Cabrillo landed here to claim land for Spain. Commerce on the bay began after the founding of the Franciscan missions in 1769. The town was annexed to Los Angeles in 1909 for the management of the port. Today **Worldport L.A.** is the busiest passenger port of call on the West Coast. You might want to go and see the dozens of fishing vessels docked at the **Fishermen's Wharf.** Another point of attraction is the **Villages at Ports o' Call**, with more than 75 unique shops and restaurants, connected by a meandering waterfront promenade. Here you can buy ultra-fresh fish in one of the shops and ask for it to be cooked for you on the spot! At the **Cabrillo Marine Aquarium** - by the very pretty **Cabrillo Beach** and right at the harbor's entrance -

you can see 38 glass tanks containing live sea animals and plants, and learn a lot about California marine environment through a series of displays. From December to April you can join, through the museum, some fascinating **whale-watch cruises**. On a peaceful knoll above the harbor, in **Angel's Gate Park**, you might want to go and see the enormous **Korean Friendship Bell**, a Bicentennial gift given by South Korea to the U.S. in 1976.

Immediately south of San Pedro, lies the other port-city of **Long Beach**, home to the **Queen Mary**, purchased for $3.5 million and still advertised as "81,000 tons of fun." Guided tours, special exhibits, musical entertainment and three restaurants constitute the main attractions of this historic vessel. From both San Pedro and Long Beach, you can reach the island of **Santa Catalina**, famous for its beautiful coves and undersea gardens. Perfect for an exciting one-day trip or a relaxing vacation throughout the year.

Yachting marina in the harbor of Long Beach.

The legendary "Queen Mary," attracting millions of visitors annually to Long Beach. Tours of the old liner, special exhibits and three restaurants are available.

View of fishing boats at the Fisherman's Wharf, on of the main attractions in San Pedro harbor. In the nearby Villages at Ports o Call, you can buy fresh fish and have it cooked in front of you.

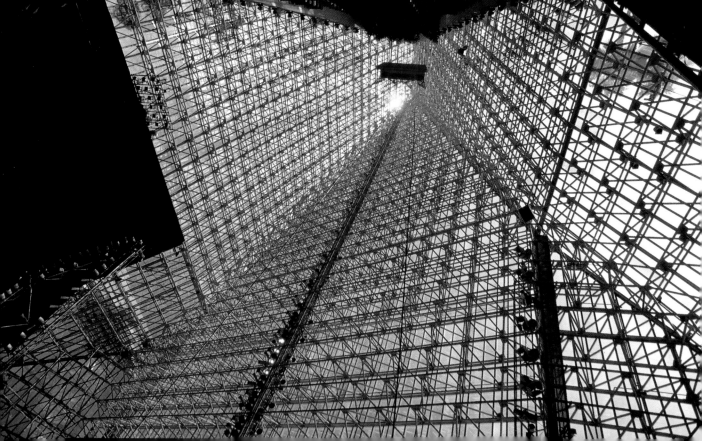

View of the Crystal Cathedral, *a unique architectural structure designed by Philip Johnson and John Burgee. Millions of people have seen it in the internationally televised religious program* Hour of Power .

The ceiling of the Crystal Cathedral. *More than 10,000 windows of tempered silver colored glass are held in place by a net of white steel trusses.*

View of the huge Anaheim Stadium, *featuring 70,000 chair-type seats.*

NORTHERN ORANGE COUNTY COMMUNITIES

South east of Long Beach, along 42 miles of coastline, between the counties of Los Angeles and San Diego, lies **Orange County**, extending 25 miles inland across residential communities, farms and orange groves. Twenty-seven miles south of Downtown L.A. is the city of Anaheim, created by German settlers in the mid -1800s. Once famous for its wineries, then for its oranges, after 1955 Anaheim became a major tourist attraction thanks to Walt Disney, who chose it as a site for his magic kingdom. But Disneyland is not the only reason to go to Anaheim. Far from it !

Originally a ten-acre fruit patch with a re-created Old West ghost town as a form of entertainment, **Knott's Berry Farm**, in the nearby community of Buena Park, today hosts almost 5 million visitors per year (it is the third theme park in the nation after Disneyland and Florida's Disney World). The expanded version contains more than 100 rides and attractions, 40 restaurants and 20 shops. A recent addition is **Camp Snoopy**, inspired by the renown comic strip character.

Very close to Anaheim, in Garden Grove, you can visit the **Crystal Cathedral**, a true architectural phenomenon. This structure has been seen by millions of people in the world thanks to the televised *"Hour of Power"* program, a creation of D.Robert H. Schuller, the visionary pastor who, in 1980, dedicated the cathedral "To The Glory of Man For The Greater Glory of God." The size of the enormous diamond-shaped building is enhanced by the all-glass covering made of more than 10,000 windows held in place by a lace-like frame of white steel trusses. The sanctuary seats 2,890 people and can house 1,000 singers and instrumentalists. Another impressive structure in the area is the **Anaheim Stadium**, built for $50 million and home to the California Angels and the L.A. Rams. The stadium seats 70,000 spectators in chair-type seats for baseball and football games.

Submarine voyage.

DISNEYLAND PARK

Millions of people from every corner of the world have discovered the fun and fantasy of Disneyland® Park, "The Happiest Place On Earth". From the old-fashioned charm of turn-of-the-century Main Street, U.S.A., to the crazy cartoon land, Mickey's Toontown, the Magic Kingdom has thrilled and delighted the young and young at heart since 1955. Disneyland features more than 60 world-famous attractions, shows and parades in eight themed lands. Wander down Main Street, U.S.A., a recreation of 19th century American town. There you can enjoy The Walt Disney Story, featuring Great Moments with Mr. Lincoln, and uncover treasures in Disneyland's many shops and boutiques. Fantasyland is home to many Disneyland classics including Pinocchio's Daring Journey, Peter Pan's Flight, Snow White's Scary Adventure and Alice in Wonderland. Streak through icy caves and treacherous blizzards on the Matterhorn Bobsleds, one of Disneyland's favorite adventures. It's thrill speed ahead in Tomorrowland's Space Mountain, a warp-speed adventure to the far reaches of the universe and Star Tours, presented by M & M's® Chocolate Candies. Are you game for fun? Then head to Adventureland and journey through untamed territory on the Jungle Cruise or climb the Swiss Family Treehouse, the treetop home of the Robinson family. Visit New Orleans Square, a famed recreation of the popular French Quarter. You'll find 999 happy haunts that are dying to meet you in the Haunted Mansion. Then it's a pirates life for you on the wildest adventure ever to rock the Spanish Main, Pirates of the Caribbean. Hungry? Choose from a variety of Louisiana specialties at the French Market or enjoy a moonlit dinner at the Blue Bayou, overlooking the Pirates of the Caribbean. Venture over to Critter Country and see your life splash before your eyes on the wild thriller; Splash Mountain. Uncover the spirited legacies of the Old West in Frontierland. Thrills and spills await on the wildest ride in the West – Big Thunder Mountain Railroad. Ready for Toons and tons of fun? Then come see how the funnier half lives in Mickey's Tootown, Disneyland's newest land in more than 20 years. It's a colorful cartoon world come to life! Catch the spark after dark with the Main Street Electrical Parade and ''Fantasy in the Sky'' Fireworks. And good battles evil in Fantasmic! Disneyland Park's newest dimension in nighttime showmanship*. Continue the fun with a stay at the 60 acre Disneyland Hotel. It's the only hotel on the Disneyland Monorail.

*Fireworks and Main Street Electrical Parade are seasonal.
Fantasmic! Weekends only during winter season.

Sleeping Beauty castle.

Mark Twain steamboat.

Splash mountain.

Arch welcoming visitors to the Newport Coast, *one of the most beautiful areas along the Pacific Ocean, south of Los Angeles.*

A peaceful morning in one of the many beaches along the Newport Coast.

A steamboat shaped restaurant in Newport Beach.

SOUTHERN ORANGE COUNTY COMMUNITIES

About 35 miles south of Downtown Los Angeles lies the beautiful seaside resort and yacht harbor of **Newport Beach**. This is one of Orange County's oldest communities and it is considered the area's high society spot 'par excellence.' Newport as such started as a small shipping center and vacation spot. Today it is a world-famous recreational community, with more than 60,000 permanent residents (summer visitors average between 20,000 and 100,000 a day). **Newport Harbor** is one of the world's busiest small boat harbors.

This resort has preserved a few interesting bits of the past. One of them is the tiny **Balboa Island Ferry**, shuttling cars and passengers between **Balboa Island** and the peninsula. The service, started in 1909, is utilized by both tourists and locals, because it cuts down driving distances and offers a better scenic view of the harbor.

The **Dory Fishing Fleet** is still operative at its turn-of-the-century **Newport Pier** location. The **Balboa Pavilion**, with its much-photographed landmark dome, has been restored in 1969, and serves as a terminal for boats going to Santa Catalina Island. Established in 1905, the Pavilion was once a fashionable location for bathing beauty contests. This was also a hot spot during the days of the big bands, and still today an annual dance, the **Balboa Hop**, is a splendid commemoration for all kind of "swingers." The Pavilion is also the setting of the annual **Flight of the Snowbirds** in Newport Harbor, the largest small boat race in the world. The first regatta took place in 1926. Now the event takes place in June and involves 150 Snowbird-class boats. **Corona del Mar** is a lovely little beach-town just south of Newport Center and site of the exquisite **Sherman Library and Gardens**. Going even further south, you will reach **Laguna Beach**. With its five-mile beach, its bays and hills, this has been described as one of the most beautiful cities in all of Southern California.

PASADENA

The landmark Beaux arts-style building of City Hall in Pasadena. The community north of Downtown Los Angeles, has retained much of its beautiful, typically Southern California architecture.

Entrance to Pasadena City Hall.

PASADENA

Defined as "the grand dame of the Greater Los Angeles area," **Pasadena** is a residential city 11 miles north-east of Downtown, right at the feet of the majestic **San Gabriel** mountain range. The Chippewa Indians called it the "crown of the valley." One of the first areas to be settled in Los Angeles, Pasadena has retained much of its original charm and beauty. **City Hall** is an example of Beaux Arts style, while many **Craftsman-style homes** can be found throughout the residential neighborhood. In recent years Pasadena, once a quiet satellite town, known primarily for its grand **Tournament Roses Parade** and the **Rose Bowl Game**, has become an important destination for great shopping and dining in the L.A. area.

South Lake Avenue between California and Colorado Boulevards is the major business and shopping district, rich in boutiques, European-flavored malls and sidewalk cafes. In this area you can visit the **Pasadena Playhouse**, an historical landmark founded in 1917 and site of the State Theatre of California. Within walking distance you can find the **Pacific Asia Museum**, with its Chinese Imperial palace architecture and a lovely courtyard garden. It was established by Grace Nicholson to introduce Pacific and Asian cultures to Southern California. You might not want to miss the nearby **Castle Green**, a unique Moorish-style building. On Colorado Boulevard, between Los Robles and Marengo, and very close to the landmark **City Hall building**, there is another shopping venue called **Plaza Pasadena**, reflecting the Spanish revival-style of the city's architecture.

West of Plaza Pasadena you can find **Old Town**

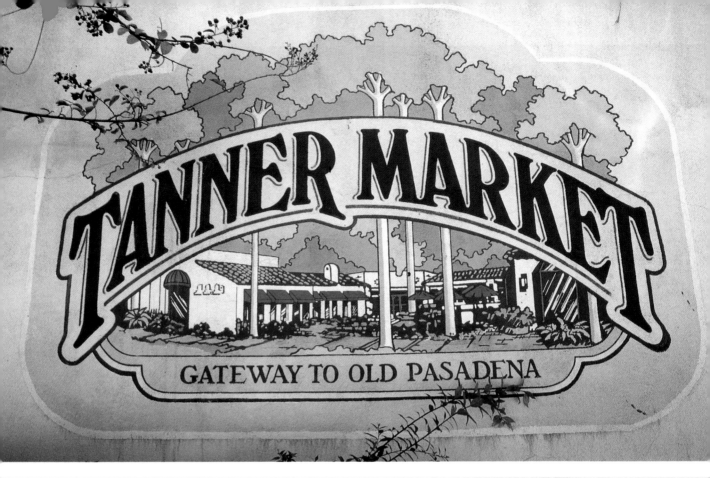

TANNER MARKET

GATEWAY TO OLD PASADENA

Sign welcoming visitors to Old Pasadena, *one of the city's main attractions, famous for its art galleries and antique shops.*

Trees and old buildings characterize the quaint neighborhood of Old Town Pasadena.

One of the many sculptures adorning the beautiful Huntington Library, Museum and Botanical Gardens *in San Marino, near Pasadena.*

Following pages: *different views of the* Botanical Gardens, *in San Marino, near Pasadena. The Botanical Gardens cover 130 acres with 15 separate sections. The most famous is probably the Desert Garden, the largest mature cacti garden in the U.S. In the background the* San Gabriel Mountains, *separating the Los Angeles Basin from the Mojave Desert to the east.*

Pasadena, covering 12 square blocks. Despite its name this is one of the artsiest and trendiest parts in the city. The best way to visit is by strolling around the neighborhood, famous for its historic buildings, picturesque alleys and sidewalk cafes. Another attractive feature is the variety of art galleries, antique shops and vintage clothing boutiques. Pasadena is also home to the **Norton Simon Museum**. Located at the western end of Colorado Boulevard, it contains important European art, from the Renaissance to the Post-Impressionist period. One of the area's most beautiful sites is definitely the

Huntington Library, Museum and Botanical Gardens, located at 1151 Oxford Road, in the nearby community of San Marino. The 207-acre estate is a legacy of its creator, pioneer railroad tycoon Henry E.Huntington (1850-1927). His mansion is now an art gallery, chiefly with English and French work from the 18th century. The **Library Exhibition Hall** is famous for its rare books and manuscripts, amongst which a copy of Gutenberg Bible from the 1450s. A real must are the Botanical Gardens. The most popular one remains the **Desert Garden**, the largest mature cacti garden in the USA.

The Santa Anita Park *racetrack, one of the most important in California. In the background the* San Gabriel mountain *range.*

The Rose Bowl, *the famous stadium near Pasadena, home to the New Year's Day football game and host to the Soccer World Cup finals in the summer of 1994.*

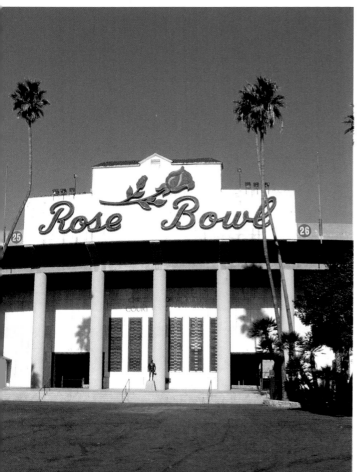

SANTA ANITA - ROSE BOWL

West of Pasadena, in **Arcadia**, always with the San Gabriel Mountains in the background, you can find the **Santa Anita Park** racetrack. Inaugurated on Christmas Day 1934, the track has played an important role in the California history of thoroughbred horse racing. During the season, visitors can watch the morning workouts, have breakfast and, on weekends, even tour the stables. Other two major racetracks in the region are **Hollywood Park**, in Inglewood, east of LAX Airport, and **Los Alamitos**, just west of Disneyland, on Katella Avenue.

In the north-eastern part of Pasadena, in beautiful **Brookside Park**, is the **Rose Bowl**, site of the celebrated football game played on New Year's Day, and host to the 1994 Soccer World Cup finals.

SIX FLAGS

In the green community of **Valencia**, some 28 miles north of Downtown, is the location of **Six Flags Magic Mountain**, another big family (and non-family) attraction competing with Disneyland, Knott's Berry Farm and Universal City. Opened in the spring of 1974, with its ponds, lakes, waterfalls and trees, "Mountain" is now one of seven Six Flags theme parks scattered throughout the nation. Here you can find over 100 attractions and rides. Amongst the biggest sensations you cannot miss **Roaring Rapids**, an adventurous whitewater river raft ride, and the monster roller-coaster called **Viper**. New additions to the park include the **High Sierra Territory**, where you can climb aboard a raft and shoot down the new Yosemite Sam Sierra Falls, and, for the little ones, **Bugs Bunny World**, an amusement park inspired by the famous cartoon character. Magic Mountain is full of cafeterias and snack-bars, yet the best food can be found at **Four Winds**, an oriental restaurant located at the summit of the park.

An image of Viper, one of the many 'monster' roller-coasters featured at the Six Flags Magic Mountain theme park. The Viper, they advertise, "will twist you upside down seven times."

THE MISSIONS

The arcade of the 'convento' in the Old Mission San Juan Capistrano. *The mission is considered the "jewel" amongst the the other ones along 'El Camino Real' (the string of missions built in Spanish dominated California after 1769).*

Traditional hand loom inside the 'convento', an indication of the complex economic activity engaged by the 'padres' and by the Indians. They used to produce blankets, soap, wine and even ironware.

Altar at the Old Mission San Juan Capistrano *chapel.*
Interior of the Old Mission San Juan Capistrano *chapel.*

THE OLD MISSION SAN JUAN CAPISTRANO

If you travel 56 miles south of L.A., you will find the little inland town of San Juan Capistrano. By now it is internationally known for **"the miracle of the swallows"**: every year on March 19 (St. Joseph's Day), the swallows return faithfully to the town . On October 23, the day of San Juan, the birds regularly leave, probably directed to some mysterious, warmer destination in South America. The town takes its name from "the jewel of the missions", the **Old Mission San Juan Capistrano.** The mission was practically "refounded" in 1776, after a disappointing start the year before. A stone church was started in 1797, but an earthquake destroyed it in 1812. Some of the swallows seem to have chosen the ruins as a nesting site. The semitropical surroundings are serene and peaceful. On the same grounds you will find the remains of what is thought to be the oldest building in California. The 17th century altar comes from Catalonia. Inside you will be welcomed by the whir of pigeons coming from a fountain named in their honor. You might want to bring with you a bag of bird food......

The semi-tropical look of the grounds surrounding the San Fernando Mission.

Peace and quiet can still be enjoyed around the fountain at the San Fernando Mission.

Detail of the 'new' chapel at San Fernando Mission.

The 21 classic arch arcade of the 'convento' in the San Fernando Mission.

MISSION SAN FERNANDO

In 1769, a Franciscan 'padre', Junipero Serra, created the first in a series of missions along 'El Camino Real' (the Royal Road). In the end the total number of missions was 21, all the way from San Diego to Sonoma, in northern California. They were seen by the king of Spain as a good bulwark against a potential Russian encroachment in the north (the czarist empire had just purchased Alaska). The missions were structured very much like communes, in which the 'padres' and the local natives prospered together thanks to their agricultural and industrial activities. The **Mission San Fernando** was established in 1797 by Father Fermin Lasuen in what then came to be known as the **San Fernando Valley**, and was its focal point throughout the 1800s. Here you can visit the 'convento,' with its classic arches and thick adobe walls, along with the chapel - a replica of the original after the damage caused by the 1971 earthquake - adorned with primitive Indian wall paintings.

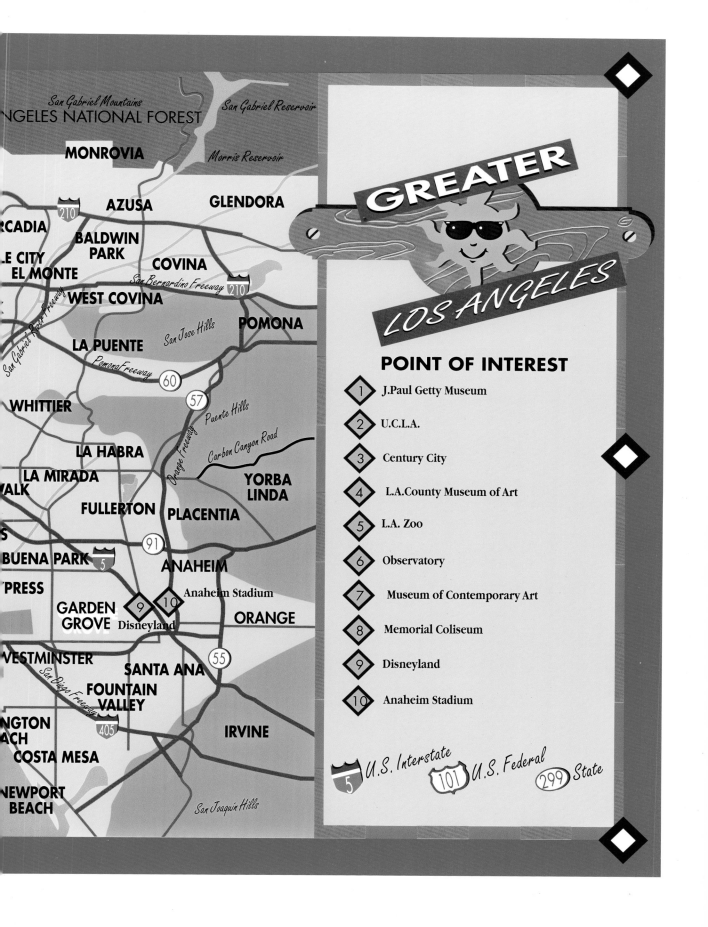

GREATER

LOS ANGELES

POINT OF INTEREST

1 J.Paul Getty Museum

2 U.C.L.A.

3 Century City

4 L.A.County Museum of Art

5 L.A. Zoo

6 Observatory

7 Museum of Contemporary Art

8 Memorial Coliseum

9 Disneyland

10 Anaheim Stadium

5 U.S. Interstate 101 U.S. Federal 299 State

San Gabriel Mountains
ANGELES NATIONAL FOREST
San Gabriel Reservoir
MONROVIA
Morris Reservoir
AZUSA
GLENDORA
RCADIA
210
BALDWIN PARK
E CITY
EL MONTE
COVINA
San Bernardino Freeway
210
WEST COVINA
San Gabriel River Freeway
San Jose Hills
POMONA
LA PUENTE
Pomona Freeway
60
57
WHITTIER
Puente Hills
LA HABRA
Carbon Canyon Road
LA MIRADA
YORBA LINDA
ALK
Orange Freeway
FULLERTON
PLACENTIA
91
BUENA PARK
5
ANAHEIM
PRESS
Anaheim Stadium
GARDEN GROVE
9
10
ORANGE
Disneyland
VESTMINSTER
55
SANTA ANA
San Diego Freeway
FOUNTAIN VALLEY
NGTON
ACH
405
IRVINE
COSTA MESA
NEWPORT BEACH
San Joaquin Hills

INDEX